Benedict Arnold: Hero and Traitor

About the Book

Benedict Arnold was brave, resourceful, and intelligent. He was one of America's earliest heroes during the difficult campaign that failed to seize Quebec. But history knows him mainly as the first important traitor to the United States. Here is the tragic story of the man who rose above an impoverished youth to glory, then fell attempting one of the shabbiest misdeeds in American history.

SPIES
OF THE
WORLD

Benedict Arnold

HERO AND TRAITOR

by Cateau De Leeuw

 G. P. PUTNAM'S SONS, NEW YORK

Foreword

There were many Americans who, like Benedict Arnold, had been dissatisfied with the way the new country's affairs were being handled. There were many who had lost fortunes in the struggle against the mother country. There were many who had suffered slights and indignities and who had not been rewarded for their efforts.

Most of them took these things in their stride. They did not scheme to betray their country. They did not have the fatal flaws of pride, ambition, and greed which were combined in Arnold to such an astonishing extent.

It is always tragic to see good material go to waste, and there was much good in Arnold. He was intelligent, brave, and resourceful. Some people have wondered if his story might not have been different if he had not been balked in his efforts and slighted by Congress. But the faults which led to his treason were part of his character from his childhood. Whether they would have been kept under control by proper recognition of his good qualities will always remain a mystery. We can only judge him now by the facts of history.

The **Spies of the World** books include:

Benedict Arnold: Hero and Traitor

1

Benedict Arnold was born in Norwich, Connecticut, in 1741. He was a bright boy, strong and agile. Dark-skinned, with startling blue eyes, he would have been noticed in any crowd of youngsters. His build was short and stocky, and he carried himself with a certain arrogance.

Many of his playmates suspected that the arrogance came from remembrance of times past. His father, a former cooper, had been a wealthy businessman, and in those days Benedict had been able to look down on poorer children. His pride had suffered a real blow when his father's business failed. His father took to drink after that, and his mother to prayer. Then Benedict was taunted by some of the boys whose parents had fawned on him before.

"Yah! Cooper's son!" they would cry. And one lad, with an ear for rhyme, would cry, "Cooper's son! Cooper's son! Lives in a tun!" until Benedict, rigid with anger, would storm after him and beat him with his fists. Many times, older boys had to pull him off his tormentors.

He did not fight smaller children; he went for the bullies, for boys bigger than he was. He was powerful for his age, and his inner rages lent him an astonishing strength. Most boys were afraid of him.

As if the family had not suffered enough, yellow fever struck Norwich when Benedict Arnold was away at school in a nearby town. Two of his sisters died. Others had died before, and now, out of the seven children his mother had had, only Benedict and Hannah were left. Hannah was younger than her brother, but already devoted to him.

Benedict was still a boy when he was apprenticed to the Lathrop brothers. Both were doctors whose main business was in apothecary supplies. Besides their shop, they had large herb gardens, worked by gardeners, with greenhouses for the more delicate plants. The Lathrops imported drugs from abroad, too, and their names were known far and wide.

Benedict's employers were wealthy and lived in a fine Georgian mansion. They had slaves to wait on them; they owned handsome horses, beautiful furniture, a library of books. Mrs. Lathrop was saddened by the loss of three children in infancy. When Benedict Arnold came to live in the Lathrop mansion, she was glad to have a young lad around.

Before he reached manhood, Benedict again knew wealth, poverty, and rich surroundings. Living with the Lathrops, his determination grew to become a rich man. Yet at this time he had nothing, being only an apprentice in the apothecary shop.

He began, of course, by doing the simplest chores. He swept out the store; he helped unpack the shipments from abroad. These shipments were not just herbs and drugs. Sometimes there were casks of fine wines from France; sometimes bolts of sheer woven Indian silks delighted him with their brilliant colors and patterns in gold threads. The Lathrops had an agent in Europe who had instructions to buy whatever seemed to be a good bargain. He sent all sorts of things, and the Lathrops, through their many connections, sold them at a good profit.

From his earliest days with the Lathrops, Benedict saw how easy it would be to make money. He saw, too, that it usually took money to make money. His mind was made up that someday he would be looked up to by the entire community as a rich man.

He was envied by other, less fortunate boys because of his life in the Lathrop household. He had always been a leader among the boys, and perhaps they felt that he had an easier life because he was braver than they were.

Strangely, he had not always been brave. When he was a young boy, Benedict often felt he was a coward. He had to force himself to do all sorts of daring things. One time when he was waiting, with other boys, at the grist mill with a load of grain to be ground into flour, he watched the huge waterwheel churning through the water. *What would it be like to ride it?* he wondered.

"Anybody who held onto that wheel would get a real ducking," the boy next to him said.

It was almost as if he had read Benedict's thoughts. He said, through stiff lips, "It wouldn't be hard to do, though."

The other boy laughed shrilly. "Dare you!" he said, when he had stopped laughing.

Benedict could feel his stomach knotting up in fear, but now he *had* to do it. With pretended nonchalance he went to the dam, climbed up onto it, and threw himself forward onto the wheel. His fingers clutched at the slippery wood. He'd never be able to hold on! But his strength was the strength of a desperate fear. Up, up, he rode to the top of the circle, then down, down, into the racing millstream.

He held his breath until the wheel came up again. As he opened his mouth and drew in a great gasp of air, he suddenly knew that he had conquered one fear. Now just for the fun of it, he rode the wheel around several times before he dived off into the water. When he swam to shore, his friends were wide-eyed with admiration and wonder.

From that time forward, Benedict conquered his fears one by one. He soon had a name for daring. When one of Norwich's houses burned, the townspeople turned out to watch. Flames rushed upward, and the firemen, with their small leather buckets, stood by helplessly.

Then someone cried out, "Look! Look up there!"

All eyes turned to stare at the roof of the flaming house. There, walking the ridgepole and looking as unconcerned as if he were strolling down the street, was Benedict Arnold!

Escapades like this soon made him master of the boys in town. The more daring the feats he accomplished, the more his fear diminished, until he felt he had conquered it forever.

He was not only brave, but inventive—he thought up pranks for the boys. He was their acknowledged leader and wonderfully skilled at sports. He rode well; he shot at the mark, as they called target shooting then, with deadly accuracy; he skated with grace and speed.

The merchants of the town watched his exploits. They thought he was wild and would need taming. On the other hand, he was "bold, enterprising, ambitious, active as lightning," as one man wrote. These were qualities that would make a successful man.

When Benedict was only fourteen, he tried to run away to war. The Lathrops stopped him that time, but he got a chance some months later. By this time the French and Indian War was in full swing. New Englanders were afraid that if Fort William Henry on Lake George fell to the French, there would be little to keep the enemy from coming down into their part of the country.

By the time the volunteers from Norwich got well started, the fort had fallen. The militia converged north of Albany—men from New York as well as New England —and milled about angrily. They wanted to chase the Canadians, and they rioted when their officers held them back.

Benedict was gone for only thirteen days, but he had had his first taste of war and found it hard to settle down to life in the Lathrop establishment. When his apprenticeship was over, the Lathrops wanted him to stay. He was intelligent and industrious, but he was ambitious, too, and his ambition did not lie in the town of Norwich. He wanted to see the world and become a rich man. Then he knew he would be looked up to, as his father had been looked up to in the old days.

Reluctantly, the Lathrops let him go. They even gave him 500 pounds as a start in his new life. Despite all the

kindnesses he had received from them, Benedict Arnold
was probably not too grateful. He was putting his past
behind him. He decided to open a store in New Haven.
The future he would make for himself, and he was
determined that it should be glorious.

Arnold liked luxury, and when he took his money and
went to London to buy stock for his new store, he was
so finely dressed that English businessmen thought he
was worth a great deal of money. Judging by his appearance, they gave him credit. Young Arnold made good
use of it, buying quantities of drugs for his apothecary
shop, buying fine books, and expensive items. When he
sailed back to America, he had more than 3,000 pounds'
worth of goods.

In New Haven he kept up this appearance of wealth.
It was not long before he had a handsome home, with
many servants. His stables held ten horses.

But his apparent prosperity was founded on mam-
moth debts. He kept going for two years, and then his
business failed. In those days debtors went to prison,
and Benedict Arnold was in jail for six weeks. Until
that time a man might linger in a debtors' prison for
years if there were no way to settle his debts. Arnold's
luck held in this, too, for a new act was passed that
allowed bankrupt men to settle for a few shillings on
the pound.

Small wonder that he should feel New Haven was

not the place for him at this time. He went back to Norwich and bought back the Arnold homestead. He installed his younger sister, Hannah, as his housekeeper, practically purring under her devoted care. Hannah adored her clever, vital brother, and did everything to please him.

She was an attractive girl, and people often wondered why she did not marry. Arnold, however, discouraged all suitors, and one time, when he discovered that Hannah was seeing a good deal of a certain Frenchman, he forbade her to see the man again.

One day he came back to his house unexpectedly and found the Frenchman there. Arnold fired his pistol as Hannah's suitor leaped out the parlor window. He did not hit the man, but the Frenchman left town. Hannah resigned herself to caring for her brother, and she never did marry.

Soon Arnold had another store in New Haven. Hannah tended it for him while he went adventuring in search of more money. There was a good market for horses in the West Indies, so Arnold bought ships and fitted them with stables belowdecks. With a full load of horses and lumber, he sailed for the West Indies and traded them for rum and other goods.

His ships were small—sloops or brigantines—and he always seemed happiest when he was in command of his own ship. He had sense enough not to fight nature and took storms and navigational difficulties in his stride. It was only when he stopped to trade and had to deal again with people that the aggressive, greedy side of his nature came to the fore.

He not only traded, but smuggled forbidden articles into the colonies as well. This was a profitable business, but a risky one, and there is little doubt that it was the risk that lent spice to the business for Arnold.

When he was twenty-six, Arnold married pretty Margaret Mansfield, daughter of a good New Haven family. Their sons, Benedict, Richard, and Henry, were born within a few years.

In any case, Arnold was not a man to be wholly concerned with his home life. He still felt resentment because he had been poor, and in almost everything he did, he was obviously trying to appear important to others.

The American Revolution was brewing. Young society men everywhere were forming companies of a military nature. In New Haven they formed a company of the Governor's Foot Guards, and Arnold was overjoyed to be asked to join them. They wore colorful uniforms, and Arnold, his blue eyes flashing, his straight, stocky body erect and soldierly, made a handsome figure. His happiness was complete when the others elected him their captain.

When news of the fighting at Lexington and Concord

reached New Haven, the townspeople reacted in two different ways. Arnold and his Foot Guards raced to the green to assemble for instructions. The older, more conservative citizens shrank from open war with England. They saw their homes, their families, their businesses threatened.

Arnold soon appeared before the committeemen of the town to ask for the keys to the powder house, so that he and his men could fight the British. The committeemen said they had voted to be neutral.

"You mean, you won't give me the keys?" Arnold demanded incredulously.

"We have voted to remain neutral," Colonel David Wooster repeated.

Arnold's voice was like cold steel when he spoke. "If you don't give us the keys, we'll break down the door."

He got the keys.

2

Everywhere, on their march to Cambridge, the Foot Guards were cheered and applauded. Their handsome uniforms gave them a smart appearance, and the precision of their marching made them stand out against the militia.

Ragged farm boys, slouching along with an easy woodsman's lope and carrying a variety of weapons, made up the militia in all too many cases. They were to prove themselves good fighters, but the people in the towns and villages through which they passed were more impressed by the Foot Guards.

Arnold got busy at once. His active brain had been scheming even on the march. He had a plan, and as soon as he could, he presented it to the Massachusetts Committee of Safety.

"Fort Ticonderoga in the province of New York," he told them, "has eighty pieces of heavy cannon, twenty brass guns—from four- to eighteen-pounders—and ten to twelve large mortars. There are plenty of small arms and a sloop on the lake. The fort is undermanned, poorly kept up, and could not hold out an hour under vigorous attack."

He knew what they were thinking, and when he was sure that the figures had sunk in, he added, "You need guns and cannon to besiege the British in Boston. This is where they are, and I can get them for you."

The committeemen liked the idea well enough, but they were afraid to make a move at first. "After all," they said to one another, "we are not *actually* at war with Great Britain." Yet they knew in their hearts that war was coming, that the colonies were ready to fight for their freedom.

Two days later they privately made Arnold a colonel and "commander in chief over a body of men not exceeding 400." He was to recruit his men farther west, capture the fort and garrison it, and bring back the precious cannon.

Nothing could have suited him better. Leaving his lieutenants to recruit men from the neighborhood, he set out with a manservant, riding hard. If it occurred to him that he could scarcely be a captain in Connecticut and a colonel in Massachusetts at one and the same time, he did not let it bother him. He relished the title of colonel. He was rising in the military world.

Unknown to him, a Connecticut man, to whom he had mentioned Ticonderoga and its possible capture, had been busy in the meanwhile. With some friends, this man had sent a militia captain who knew Fort Ticonderoga north to recruit men for the same project. The captain had enlisted the support of the Green Mountain Boys, a wild group of mountaineers and backwoodsmen under the leadership of a huge man, Ethan Allen. They all were great fighters.

Fort Ticonderoga was in New York territory, and these men were from that part of the country which would later become Vermont. They hated all "Yorkers," and thought it would be great fun to storm a fortress in New York province. With unanimous consent, they set out and were at a tavern some 20 miles from Ticonderoga when Benedict Arnold walked in on them.

Bearded and noisy, more than half-drunk, the Green Mountain Boys stared at the short, neat, handsomely uniformed man who told them calmly that he was to be their leader. Their answers were loud guffaws.

Arnold showed them his Massachusetts commission, which only made them laugh louder. Some of their leaders did talk with him a little, but there was small chance of their accepting him, he realized. So he set off to find their commander, Ethan Allen.

The two men did not like each other from the beginning. However, each recognized leadership qualities in the other. Before long, they had made a compromise. They would be joint commanders of the force that was to take Fort Ticonderoga.

By May 10, 1775, they had reached the shores of Lake Champlain. A mile away, across the water, was the somber fort. It was evening, and they had hoped to storm the fort at night. But there were no boats to ferry them across the water.

Not until the middle of that night did they locate some boats. They had hardly located them when the heavens opened and the skies rumbled and glared in a fierce thunderstorm. It took a long time to ferry men across. When dawn was nearly upon them, they dared not wait for their full force. Only about eighty-five men had been ferried over by this time, but if the fort were to be surprised, they could not wait for daylight.

Silently, the woodsmen slunk through the trees along the bank of the lake. When they reached a little path that led steeply upward to the fort atop the cliff, both Arnold and Allen let out a shout and began to run. Each one wanted to be the first to reach the fort.

Luck was with them. The little wicket gate at the end of the path was open. A sleepy sentry, suddenly roused by the noise, tried to shoot, but his gun misfired, and he turned and ran. A second sentry was slashed by Ethan

Allen's sword and captured. Behind Arnold and Allen, the other men came dashing upward to the fort.

No one was in sight. Everything was quiet. Arnold told the men to secure the garrison, and Allen beat on the door of the commanding officer's house, yelling, "Come out, you damned skunk, or I will sacrifice the entire garrison!"

A lieutenant heard them and tried to wake the commanding officer. That gentleman had evidently drunk too many toasts the night before and continued snoring peacefully. The lieutenant, wearing his coat but only carrying his trousers, raced down to the parade ground.

He looked from Allen to Arnold and back again. Behind them, their ragged soldiers yelled and brandished their weapons. He stared again at the two men who seemed to be in command—one an obvious backwoodsman, the other in impeccable uniform.

"By what authority have you entered the fort?" the British lieutenant asked.

Ethan Allen threw back his head and laughed. Before Arnold could reply, he said, "In the name of the Great Jehovah and the Continental Congress!"

After the commandant was awakened, there was nothing for him to do but hand them his sword and surrender the fort. The garrison had been caught abed; their arms had been taken from them without a fight.

It was a remarkable capture of a fortress that had seemed impossible to take.

Unfortunately, the Green Mountain Boys reacted to victory in their natural fashion, ransacking the fort, appropriating everything which struck their fancy. What they didn't want they destroyed.

Benedict Arnold was furious. He had promised the prisoners decent treatment, but Allen and his men only laughed when he tried to make them stop their looting. When he protested, some of the backwoodsmen shot at him, but they were usually too drunk to take good aim.

One of the men even shoved his musket against Arnold's chest and said, "You back down from your high horse, see? Ethan Allen's our leader, and you're nothin' but a popinjay that come along for the fun."

"I was commissioned to lead the attack on this fort, and I did so," Arnold replied in a steady voice. "I am *not* backing down."

The man lowered his gun and walked off, muttering something about "another swig o' rum," and Arnold took a deep breath. It had been a close call.

But although he continued to act as if he were the actual commander of the American force, no one listened to him. His attempts at order failed. He began to wonder how on earth he was going to get the promised cannon to Cambridge. The guns were there, but he knew he would never get this rabble to transport them.

Four days later he was able to breathe freely again. A schooner was sighted on the lake, and when it drew near, he found there were fifty men aboard who had been recruited by the lieutenants he had left behind him in Massachusetts.

Arnold, an experienced seaman, set about arming the schooner with some of the captured cannon. He knew there was a British naval sloop somewhere on the lake, and he was going to go after it.

The Green Mountain Boys watched him with frowning faces. They knew nothing about sailing a ship of that size, but they were determined not to be left behind. If they had anything to say about it, Arnold was not going to get all the credit for capturing the British sloop. When he sailed off down the lake, they followed in bateaux. But, no matter how hard they rowed, they could not keep up with the schooner, which had a favoring wind.

The wind died when Arnold was still 30 miles from St. Johns in Canada, where there was a fort and where, he was sure, the British sloop must be. He took some of his men in rowboats and crossed the border to surprise the British.

Learning that they were expecting reinforcements at any time, he captured the sloop, with its two brass cannon, and set about destroying all the military matériel he could not take with him. The whole affair went very quickly, and Arnold sailed off in the sloop, towing his two rowboats. Some distance down the lake he met the Green Mountain Boys, still rowing doggedly.

"It's no use, Boys," he called out. "The job's done!" Then he saluted them with his new cannon. The Boys fired a salute in return, and when he shouted, "We've rum on board!" there was a mad scramble to board the sloop.

He told them about the expected reinforcements at St. Johns, but that did not deter the Boys. "We'll take it again and hold it!" they shouted as they rowed away toward Canada.

The Boys came back to Ticonderoga four days later. The British reinforcements had surprised them as they slept near St. Johns. By this time most of them decided that they had had enough of war. After all, they were needed at home, they said, and many of them left.

Arnold had a difficult time. Because the colonies were not officially at war with England, their mother country, the various legislatures of the colonies were afraid to praise him for his work. Worse still, no one wanted to take the blame for having let him lead an attack on a British fort. The congresses of Connecticut and Massachusetts seesawed back and forth, sometimes praising, sometimes condemning him for his actions.

He learned to disregard most of this, but it must have made him bitter. The very men who had so desperately wanted the cannon he sent them and who had accepted them for the siege of Boston now reproached him for having taken them from a British fort. They decided that the cannon were only "borrowed." Arnold must have laughed when he heard that.

In the meantime he had trained his recruits, had found a ruined fort farther north on an island in Lake Champlain and had kept his little fleet there at the ready in case of invasion. He himself went north, dreaming of something that might possibly be accomplished by a determined force of men and a leader like himself: the capture of Canada.

Canada had belonged to the British Crown for only twelve years. It had been a French possession, and the inhabitants were still largely French, many of them antagonistic to the English. When the British conquerors, in order to disturb conditions in Canada as little as possible, had wooed the large landholders, the majority of the Canadians were in as bad a situation as they had been under the French king—perhaps worse!

Arnold hoped to make use of this discontent. With the support of the inhabitants, he felt an invasion could be successful. He interviewed some the people, sent a man to feel out the Indians of the region, and began to make plans.

By the time he sent these plans to the Continental Congress, they were fully detailed. Always a schemer,

Arnold saw himself the conqueror of a vast territory. He would be remembered in history. He would be able to bask in the fame of his exploits.

On his way back to Cambridge to settle his accounts, he stopped at his home. Now, surely, his wife would appreciate him, would realize that she had married a hero! It was his sister, Hannah, who came to meet him in a strangely silent house. Margaret, his wife, she told him quickly, had died while he had been gone.

Dreams of glory came to earth with this sad news. Hannah had more bad news, although she tried to tell him as gently as she could. His business had suffered since he left to go to war. The brigantine he had sent to Quebec would surely be confiscated by the British now. He would have to get a cargo for the brig that was coming soon from the West Indies.

To add to his miseries, he fell ill with gout and had to keep to his bed. Small wonder that there were times when black despair washed over him in a drowning wave.

3

While he was still at Ticonderoga, Arnold had sent a detailed plan to Congress for an invasion of Canada. Most Americans, however, were still not ready for a complete break with England, and anything like an invasion could only be classed as open war.

It was not until later that year, when General George Washington feared that reinforcements would soon be sent across the Atlantic to Quebec, that any move toward Canada was set in motion. It was Washington's idea that if an army could suddenly appear before Quebec—an army that had taken a route through thick forest country—the citadel might be surprised.

The obvious leader for such an expedition was Benedict Arnold, and his eager response, when Washington approached him about it, reassured the great general.

The route the invading army was to take was known only to a few traders, missionaries, and Indians. Since even the Indians were afraid of it and avoided it if possible, this should have been a warning. But Washington, anxious for some positive action, did not realize what the trip would entail.

As for Arnold, he was delighted to have the chance to prove himself a hero. The past months had been wearisome and infuriating. The capture of Ticonderoga had cost him so much from his own pocket that he felt impoverished. Yet when he tried to get the Massachusetts Committee of Safety to pay him for the items which he had bought for the Army, they argued and haggled and beat him down in his price until he had a very low opinion of political figures.

Now he was a colonel in the Continental Army and would have only Army superiors. More than 1,000 men enlisted for the venture. Some of them were the famous riflemen under Colonel Daniel Morgan. All of these were experienced men in the woods, but others were not nearly so well prepared for the trip.

They set out in the middle of September and found the 200 bateaux that had been ordered for them at the Kennebec River. The bateaux were badly made of green lumber.

"They'll leak like sieves," Arnold said in disgust to his friend and secretary, Eleazer Oswald. "We'll have a time keeping our powder dry—not to mention our provisions."

He looked up at the gray sky. Leaky bateaux or no, he would have to get started soon. Winter snows might force him back if he waited to have other boats made.

Their route took them through unexplored country. Forests and mountains and streams made the traveling difficult. They could not go directly but had to leave the Kennebec far up and cross three ponds (really lakes), with portages between them, before they could reach Dead River. This was called the Great Carrying Place.

Arnold saw to the departure of the men each day. Then, when all were on their way, he was to start up-river in a canoe paddled by strong Indians. In this way he could spot trouble along the route, could help the sick or stragglers, and, once he had reached the men in the lead, could wait for the others to come up again. He kept an eye on everyone and everything.

By the time they reached Dead River, they had been almost a month in the wilderness. Arnold's plan was to get to the Chaudière River and follow it down to the St. Lawrence. It would land him and his men across the great river from Quebec.

But now their food was getting low. The leaky bateaux had spoiled some of the provisions; accidents on the difficult portages had destroyed still more. There was no way to replenish the stores, for there were no settlements within many miles, and game had been frightened away by such a large body of men.

In spite of this, they had been lucky so far. But now their luck changed. It began to rain, steadily, fiercely. The Dead River rose and rose, made higher by huge quantities of driftwood that came washing down from higher up. The men were soaked; their spare clothing was soaked; their powder was wet; their food was spoiled. Although they stayed on higher ground, the river gave no signs of subsiding. Finally, they went on for a short distance, but they lost a number of their bateaux in the raging waters.

It was then that Arnold decided to hold a conference with his officers. They were short of boats; their ammunition was low; their food was practically gone. Winter was coming on rapidly in this northern country; ice was already forming along the banks of the stream. Many of the advance men were weakened by exposure and sickness. These were the facts he laid before them. Should they turn back?

Arnold could not bear the thought of retreat, yet he had to consult with his men. About half his little army had not yet come up to him—the men under Colonels Roger Enos and Christopher Greene. He could not wait for them; at this time of year every day counted. Should they go on or turn back?

There were undoubtedly officers who felt that to go

on was foolhardy, yet Arnold had powers of persuasion. He was cautious enough in preparation for trouble, but when trouble struck, his instinct was to do the unexpected—to strike back. It was good psychology where human beings were concerned, but nature is not influenced by such tactics. Cold and starvation would not heed him.

He planned carefully for the sick. They were to be sent back. And he gave leave to any of the others who did not want to go on to return with them. The men voted to go on, sure that with such a leader they could not fail.

The sick came back down the river where Colonel Enos was waiting fearfully for news of the advance party. Their stories of the hardships ahead were frightening, and a bad snowstorm helped weaken Enos' resolve. He turned back with a quarter of the little army. Worst of all, he took most of the provisions that remained with him.

Colonel Greene went ahead with his men, but long before he reached the main body of the army, Arnold had left. He had sent a captain with forty good woodsmen to hunt for the nearest French settlement. They were to buy whatever provisions were to be had. Then Arnold decided to go with them, for the food question was all-important.

This advance group now had to find a way through

35

a dreadful part of the country, and the men had no maps. Ponds, rivers, swamps, and bogs appeared in every direction. Following a stream that looked promising might lead in an entirely wrong direction, and a great deal of time was wasted in this way. There were steep declivities to bypass, fallen trees to hamper their progress.

They were always hungry; they were never dry. There weren't enough boats anymore. At every one of the rapids and waterfalls more of the bateaux had been wrecked, more of the men soaked in clothing that soon froze on them. But they knew they must be getting closer to the French settlements, and they had found no outposts of British troops to give away the surprise they hoped for.

On the third day they saw smoke from a cabin. Soon a farm came into view—a farm with cattle! Arnold ran to the farmer, money in his hand. The first provisions had been found! From now on it would be easy to find food for his men.

Back in the wilderness, his little army suffered days of frightful hardship. Many of the men died, and many more grew too weak to go on. There was absolutely *nothing* to eat. The men boiled their moccasins and chewed on them to ease their hunger pangs. They killed and ate the pet dogs that had been with them.

When they reached the Chaudière River, they knew

4

On a moonless night, in silent birchbark canoes, a large portion of Arnold's raggedy forces paddled across the river, avoiding the British men-of-war and their patrol boats. A few days later they were joined by most of the rest of the men.

Arnold needed more troops before he could attack Quebec, and he wrote for reinforcements. He hoped they would hurry, because the enlistments of the men under him would expire on December 31.

General Richard Montgomery, having cleared Lake Champlain of the British, had gone, under orders to Montreal, which he had taken quite easily. He came down the St. Lawrence to Quebec with all the men he could spare from garrisoning Montreal. Although they were welcome, they were pitiably few.

Montgomery, being a general, was in command, but he had great respect for Arnold's initiative and decisiveness. Both men agreed that the only way they could hope to take Quebec would be on a snowy night, when the falling snow would hide them.

Now the wait began. Once they started out, but the air cleared too soon. The end of the year crept closer and closer, and Arnold was afraid that with the new year he would lose most of the men under his command.

On the night of December 31, 1775, the snow came. With Montgomery leading the attack on one side and Arnold on the other, they hoped to scale the steep sides of the fortress after winding up the narrow, twisting streets of the Lower Town that led to it.

Disaster struck almost at once—with the first cannon shot from the British, who saw a few shadowy figures emerge from the snowy landscape. General Montgomery was killed. Many of his officers fell, too. The soldiers panicked; some of them ran back. Others were lost without the orders of their officers.

On Arnold's side of the fortress, they made better progress, but Arnold was struck in the leg by a bullet. Although he stood leaning against a wall and directing the others, he soon had to be helped to the rear. Even then, on the way, he urged his men to the attack. "Rush on, brave boys! Rush on!" he cried.

Morgan's riflemen scaled the barracade, and those who could followed. But there was no leadership for either attacking party. The British were well aroused by this time. Many of the Americans, including some of

40

Arnold's best officers, were made prisoners. All the rest who had been in Arnold's detachment were killed. The other troops retreated.

It was a crushing defeat. If the British had sallied out of their fortress, they could have taken the entire attacking American army with ease. Perhaps they thought the Americans were stronger than they were and did not realize that they were leaderless and starving. Arnold lay in a Catholic hospital, unconscious during the first hours of complete defeat, later recovering slowly from his wound.

Some of the men, their enlisted time up, simply went home. Others, weakened by their long ordeal, succumbed to smallpox which raged through the camp. Arnold now had fewer than 500 men who could possibly fight. Strangely, he did not seem too discouraged.

Benedict Arnold was made a brigadier general in January, 1776. He asked to be made commandant of Montreal, and his request was granted. It was there that he began to have trouble with the Canadians, who had at first appeared sympathetic. Now they were turning against him and his men. The Americans had no money to pay for supplies—only the worthless paper money of the Continental Congress. When the Canadians refused to part with supplies for payment in this money, the Americans often resorted to force. Former friends became enemies.

Arnold knew he would have to leave Montreal soon, and he began gathering merchandise for the army without paying the Canadian merchants. He sent it to St. Johns, to be held there until everything could be listed and accounted for. Unfortunately, the commander at St. Johns did not like Arnold. He did not set a guard over the bales of goods that arrived from Montreal. When Arnold got there, the packages had been ransacked—a great deal had been stolen—and no one seemed to know who had done it or what had been in the bales. The Canadian merchants got nothing.

Some of the officers said that Arnold had made a lot of money in this situation. It is possible, because he had, in his business life, not been too honorable where debts and payments were concerned. This dishonest attitude remained with him all his life and was, undoubtedly, one of the main reasons for his downfall.

General John Sullivan was sent to take charge in Canada, but it was obvious that Canada was lost to the rebelling colonies. The retreat of the main army to St. Johns was disorderly, yet Arnold's men still kept their discipline. They set St. Johns afire, watched it burn, and were the last to leave.

Arnold realized, as did the other military leaders, that the gateway for the British and Canadians into New England and New York was Lake Champlain. Once more Arnold took on the defense of the lake. Boats had to be built, but he had no shipbuilders. He had to teach men how to build them. There was no rigging and no material for it. All that had to be shipped from the seacoast.

He had no sailors when the boats were finished. He had to train men in the simplest tasks of sailing. Yet as always when he was battling against odds and over- coming innumerable difficulties, Arnold was quite cheerful. His confidence was infectious, and the men under him worked hard to please him.

The British had ships already built; they had quan- tities of materials for the building of new ones. They had experienced workmen and sailors. Arnold knew they would be coming soon, and he had to work against time.

To make matters worse, news kept coming in of American defeats. Although Washington had made good use of the cannon Arnold had sent him from Ticon- deroga and had driven the British from Boston, he had lost battles on Long Island and on Manhattan. There had been one surprising victory at Harlem Heights, but the Americans were in retreat, a fact which could not be denied.

Arnold took his little fleet as far north on Lake Cham- plain as he dared. At Valcour Island there was a narrow channel. There he hid his little collection of boats be- hind the island, waiting for the British naval invasion.

It came on October 11, 1776, and for two days his

little navy fought valiantly, trying to stem the southward passage of the British ships. It was a very uneven conflict. The British sailors were old hands at warfare on the water; their officers were trained and experienced.

Against the astonishing number of British ships, Arnold's little fleet fought gallantly until there was nothing left of it. Arnold and a few of his men blew up the last of their ships and managed to escape to the west shore of the lake. From there they made their way to Ticonderoga.

Military mistakes were made on both sides in the American Revolution. Opportunities for victory were sometimes lost or ignored or overlooked, and this was one of them. If the British General Guy Carleton, after his victory on Lake Champlain, had continued south, he could have taken Fort Ticonderoga with ease. Then the new country would have been divided into two parts, with New England on one side and New York and the more southern colonies on the other. The Revolution would have had to peter out. Without help from one another, the individual colonies could not have withstood the enemy.

Yet for some unknown reason, Carleton did not follow up his remarkable advantage. Instead, he turned back to Canada. By their show of aggression and determined bravery, Arnold and his men had perhaps discouraged the British leader. Whatever it was, the country was safe again, for a while, in that area.

5

When there was no fighting, Arnold was at a loose end and, sooner or later, got into trouble with other officers. He was pleased and flattered when aristocratic General Philip Schuyler was friendly to him. He did not take sides at first in the military feud that developed between Schuyler and General Horatio Gates, who was appointed to lead the northern armies. He was on good terms with both, but his natural leanings were toward the wealthy and aristocratic Schuyler.

There was a good deal of self-seeking, even in the Patriot Army. There was always a scramble to get credit after an engagement. Arnold, more than most, felt the need for praise and advancement. He could not forget the years in which he had been a nobody, and his pride made him ache for recognition.

Arnold felt he had accomplished a wonderful feat in his invasion of Canada. That he had been defeated hardly mattered. Hadn't he led men through an almost impassable wilderness? Hadn't he inspired them to extraordinary deeds of bravery? Hadn't he been wounded himself in the attack on Quebec? Hadn't he fought against great odds on Lake Champlain?

With all this filling his mind, he was completely floored when Congress raised five juniors officers to the rank of major general. This was a terrible slight. These men had been below him in rank; now they were above him. He felt there was only one thing he could do—resign.

Yet he hated the thought. Fighting was in his blood. He was never happier than when he was leading men in an attack, encouraging them by his own reckless bravery. If he resigned, he would be out of the war. He would be a civilian again, and that would be intolerable.

He demanded a court of inquiry, sure that someone or several "someones" had been maligning him. Actually, Congress thought of him as a brave man who deserved a higher rank than brigadier general, but Congress was afraid of offending certain colonies. There were already too many generals from Connecticut. Some of the other colonies were protesting that they were not properly represented in the command of the Army.

Perhaps it was his first blow from Congress that began

to turn Arnold from the fierce patriot he had been (always, of course, with an eye to his own advancement and credit) into a man who eyed the political side of war before he went into action.

The change did not come at once. He was still to be the impulsive fighter, the courageous leader, the rallier of frightened men when he was in battle. But his feelings had been wounded deeply. He felt that nothing he accomplished was appreciated. Certainly, he was now tempted to put self above country.

To make matters worse, a young Tory beauty whom he had courted when in Boston some months previously turned him down for a mere civilian! Arnold went home to his sister, Hannah, and brooded.

A pounding on his door one morning before dawn brought back his old alertness. The messenger told him that a British force had landed near Norwalk, Connecticut, and marched inland. Arnold was dressed and mounted in record time. He and old General David Wooster rode fast, gathering militia as they went. Before they got to Danbury, the reddening sky told them that the town was in flames.

Arnold and Wooster quickly agreed on a plan. Wooster would attack the British rear as they marched back to the shore. Arnold would block them in front. This meant a forced march for the 500 men under Arnold, in order to get ahead of the British, but they reached the narrow place near Ridgefield that he had in mind.

The road was squeezed there between a big farmhouse and a rocky ledge. This was where he and his men built a barricade. Farm wagons, chairs, and loose logs were piled on top of one another to stop the British.

And then, around the bend of the road, the British appeared, marching in order, three abreast. Cannon were brought forward and fired at the barricade. Arnold, on his big horse, rode from side to side, encouraging his militia, and they held fast until someone looked up and saw Hessian soldiers atop the cliff on their left.

The militia ran. Arnold stayed behind to keep their retreat in some order, and thirty Hessians on the cliff fired at him. His horse fell heavily, struck by eight bullets, and Arnold could not leap free, for his foot was caught in the stirrup. He was thrown facedownward in the mud.

A Tory soldier came running, aiming his bayonet at Arnold, who, at the last possible moment, managed to raise his pistol.

"Not yet!" he shouted, and shot the man dead. Then he ran for cover in the swamp, with bullets and grapeshot missing him as if by a miracle. His hat was riddled with holes from the bullets, but he was untouched.

Somehow, he got another horse and rode through the

countryside, trying to gather together more men. He had only 250 when his friend Oswald arrived with three cannon. Wooster, he learned, had been killed. The British, moving slowly and cautiously after the skirmish at Ridgefield, had not yet reached Norwalk Harbor, where their transports were.

Arnold saw that the British would have to cross the river to get to their ships, and he stationed his men along the banks of the Saugatuck. His cannon shot at the first division of British to appear, and a second shot threw them into some disorder. But British soldiers were well disciplined. They crossed the river higher up, so that Arnold had to order his men to cross, too.

The militia that had been with General Wooster caught up with him at this time and joined the men. They harassed the British until they came to the harbor, but there fresh British troops were landed from the ships to fight them.

At this, the militiamen broke. They did not listen as Arnold pleaded with them to stay and fight. He rode out alone, thinking he was leading a charge, only to find he was facing the British Army all by himself. Undismayed, he turned his back on the British and tried once more to rally his troops. They had had enough of fighting, so that in the end he had to retreat, too.

Although he had met defeat again, his personal fortunes were in better condition. Congress could not ignore this latest exploit and finally made him a major general. Unfortunately, seniority still ruled in the Army, so that he would be compelled to serve under those who had received the rank earlier.

General Washington wrote in his behalf, "It is needless to say anything of this gentleman's military character. It is universally known that he has always distinguished himself as a judicious, brave officer of great activity, enterprise and perseverance."

In spite of this praise, Congress still refused to change its mind in the matter of seniority. But it did vote him a horse with trappings for his "gallant conduct during the Danbury invasion." This was small recognition, Arnold felt, and when one of his former officer enemies, John Brown, published thirteen charges against him, Arnold's anger flared.

His name was cleared in the end, but he was no farther up the ladder of military success. This was one more thing to gnaw at his self-pride. He resigned from the Army.

6

Arnold was secretly relieved when he received no acknowledgment of his resignation. He really could not bear the thought of retiring to civilian life while a war was going on and while there was the chance to achieve renown and, possibly, money.

General "Gentleman Johnny" Burgoyne, a British commander, was leading troops steadily south from Canada through New York State. If General William Howe sailed up the Hudson with his troops and the two met at Albany, the country would be cut in two. It was the same danger that had threatened with Ticonderoga; only this time it was even more serious.

Burgoyne had plenty of Indian allies, but they were hard to control. Indians did not take to discipline. They did not want to wait for the long chance. They wanted to fight; they wanted loot and scalps. As the British troops advanced, the Indians got more and more out-of-hand.

Soon there were horrifying stories of burning and scalping, of murdered men, women, and children in the outlying districts. These stories came down to American headquarters in Albany, where General Schuyler was commander. There was nothing to stop the wildly advancing Indians but a small fort near present-day Utica, called Fort Stanwix.

German settlers of the region gathered under the leadership of a farmer, Nicholas Herkimer. They were going to the relief of Fort Stanwix when they were ambushed by the Indians at Oriskany. In the bloody battle that followed, the farmers were defeated. Now there was practically nothing in the way of marauding Indians. The settlers were panic-stricken.

"Let me go," Arnold said. He was sure that he could raise a force of militia and settle the troubles of the frontier.

Arnold was given 900 men and set out. At German Flats, a small settlement, he settled down with his soldiers and began recruitment. The militia of the area were so frightened that they would not volunteer. The friendly Indians that Arnold had counted on did not appear.

He did not dare move against the enemy. He was

completely outnumbered and realized that a battle at this point could only result in defeat for the Americans. While he waited at German Flats, uncertain whether to advance or retreat, two prisoners were brought in to him. They had been recruiting soldiers for the British behind the American lines and had been sentenced to death.

One of the men, an apparent lunatic, was named Hon Yost Schuyler. He twitched his arms and legs, rolled his eyes, and spoke in strange animallike sounds. His brother, the other prisoner, was normal enough. While Arnold was interviewing them, their mother rushed in and threw herself on her knees before him, begging for her sons' lives.

These people had lived so long on the frontier that they had forgotten many of their white ways. They were more Indian than white by now, and this suddenly gave Arnold an idea. He remembered that crazy people were looked up to by the Indians, who thought they were able to communicate with the Great Spirit.

Arnold looked at Hon Yost and decided that there was a spark of sanity visible at times. He made up his mind.

"Could you scare off the Indian allies of the British?" he asked the madman.

A sly look stole over Hon Yost's face. His limbs

stopped their twitching. "Yes," he answered. "It would be easy."

Soon it was agreed that he would try. If he succeeded, Arnold would pardon him and his brother. The Indians knew he had been captured. It was arranged that he would make some bullet holes in his clothing to show that he had barely escaped the Americans, and then he would tell the Indians about the tremendous power and size of the American Army.

Hon Yost's brother was locked up as a hostage, and the madman set out for the Indian camp. He found the Indians in the middle of an angry powwow. They were dissatisfied with the British, who had left most of the fighting at Oriskany to them. To make matters worse, when the Indians had left their camp in front of Fort Stanwix to fight the Americans at Oriskany, the Americans had sallied out of the fort and taken all their belongings.

Now the British were urging them to ambush Arnold and his men, and they wanted none of it. Arnold was known as a powerful fighting man, and the Indians were wary of him.

At this point Hon Yost ran up to the council fire, screaming. He talked wildly, making his strange animal sounds for quite a while, and the Indian braves sat silent, waiting for a message from the Great Spirit. At last the madman's words began to make sense. He said the Americans were as numerous as the leaves on the trees, and the Indians should run from them. An Indian friend of Hon Yost's came on the scene then, with wampum from Arnold, and said that Arnold's quarrel was with the British, not with the Indians.

The Indians went to Barry St. Leger, the British commandant, and told him they wanted to retreat at once. When St. Leger refused to go along with them, they grew quite wild. They snatched at the liquor in the British camp. Once it had been drunk, they became threatening. The British thought it was wisest to obey their furious allies and went at once, leaving their tents and cannon standing. The Indians, even then, tried to hurry them along and rode around them whooping and shouting and killing any who did not come fast enough.

The men in Fort Stanwix were at a complete loss to explain this sudden retreat of their besiegers. But once the British and the Indians had disappeared, Hon Yost walked up to the fort and yelled, "General Arnold is coming!"

Arnold, afraid of Indian ambushes, had come only a little way when he received word of the relief of Fort Stanwix. His sudden inspiration concerning Hon Yost had paid him well. Without the loss of a man, he had sent the British and their Indian allies into ignominious retreat.

He was proud of his success and fully expected that

Congress would, at last, recognize his worth. He thought his seniority over former junior officers would be restored, but Congress thought otherwise.

7

General Gates was commander in the north when Arnold returned from his expedition to the Mohawk Valley. Gates, who had taken the place of General Schuyler, Arnold's friend, had decided on a policy of slowing down Burgoyne's advance by cutting his supply line and starving the British out, if possible.

Burgoyne's men—both British and German—were soon hungry. There was food in Vermont to the east. The German dragoons had no horses, and there were horses to be had in Vermont. Burgoyne sent out a task force under Lieutenant Colonel Friedrich Baum to bring in food and horses and cattle. It made such slow progress, being hampered by heavy equipment and cannon, that the Hampshire men, with a few hundred from Massachusetts, had time to gather and attack.

Baum's men were terribly defeated at Bennington, and a second force, sent to their relief, had to retreat ignominiously, with the Americans sniping at them constantly.

Arnold, returning in triumph from Fort Stanwix, was surprised that Gates had not followed up this success with an immediate attack on Burgoyne's main army. Gates scarcely listened to him. Arnold had noticed a change in Gates' attitude at once and was both hurt and angry. He did not realize that Gates still thought highly of his fighting prowess but considered him too impulsive.

In the middle of September, 1777, Burgoyne crossed to the west side of the Hudson River. He was still determined to get to Albany, even though he must have realized that General Howe would not be there to meet him. The three-pronged attack that had been planned—under Burgoyne, St. Leger, and Howe—was hopeless now. St. Leger had been defeated at Fort Stanwix; Howe was in Philadelphia; only Burgoyne was left.

The British Army felt its way southward for several days, through woods and over rugged hills. When they reached the abandoned Freeman farm, with cleared fields, the English general was relieved. Here, at last, was a decent place for a battle. The British did not like the kind of pioneer fighting that was modeled partly on Indian tactics. They wanted an open space where neat lines of soldiers could march abreast into battle.

Burgoyne divided his men into three parts. He remained in the center, General Simon Fraser went by a path to the western fields of the Freeman farm, and General Friedrich von Riedesel, the German commander, took the river road. They knew that they would be meeting the Americans soon. Distant drumming told them that the American Army was near.

Arnold commanded the left wing of the Patriot Army. He was elated at the thought of battle again. He knew instinctively that this was the field in which he shone. At American headquarters he urged an all-out attack. Gates, as always more cautious than Arnold, did not believe that his whole command should leave the protection of its entrenchments.

It was Daniel Morgan's Pennsylvania rifle corps which began a battle that raged forward and back that day. With the British officers in front falling before the accurate fire of the Pennsylvanians, there was soon a retreat. Then Morgan's men rushed forward to try to turn the British cannon against them. This delay gave the enemy enough time to rally. They came running at the Americans with their bayonets at the charge, and the riflemen fled in their turn.

Back and forth for more than three hours the battle raged. The gold of the ripe wheat was stained with red and trampled fiercely as the opposing forces fought.

Then the German troops came to the rescue of the British, and the Americans returned to their encampment.

Arnold had paced furiously during the engagement. Once he started off toward the action on his big horse, but Gates recalled him. Arnold wanted to be out there where the fighting was. He wanted to be on his mount, his sword held aloft, leading his men. The thrill that came to him in battle was like meat and drink to him. And here he was, tied to "Granny" Gates' apron strings!

The ill feeling that sprang up between the two men that day never died down. From then on they were enemies, although they fought in the same army. Gates, remembering that Arnold had sent in his resignation, treated him as if he were a guest at the camp, but not a welcome guest. He gave him no power, while Arnold continued to act as if the Americans' left wing were still under his command. The situation was ridiculous, as well as dangerous.

Knowing, from reports, that Burgoyne was digging in at Bemis Heights near the Freeman farm, Arnold urged attack before the British could be too sheltered behind their redoubts. But Gates still pursued his wait-and-starve-them-out policy. *He* knew, from his reports, that the British had practically no supplies left and that Sir Henry Clinton in New York could not reach Burgoyne in time with reinforcements and supplies.

On October 7 there was action at last. Burgoyne, desperate by this time, drew up his battle lines at Freeman's farm again.

Messengers rode wildly from the field of battle to General Gates with news from the front. Arnold, stalking about like a caged lion and completely ignored by his commander, was raging. He only heard snatches of reports. Enoch Poor's brigade had stormed up a steep slope and put the British grenadiers to flight. Dan Morgan and his men were attacking the British right. But none of this news was being relayed to Arnold.

Frantic at being out of the action, Arnold suddenly sprang onto his mount and raced toward the battlefield. Gates was furious and sent Major John Armstrong after him, but Arnold was riding a powerful horse.

Hardly pausing in his wild charge, except to call to the soldiers, "Come on, brave boys, come on!" Arnold dashed straight at the enemy.

As always, the men responded to his personal bravery and followed him, cheering. The British lines hardly wavered. Turning to see how his men were faring, Arnold found that they were in retreat from the Hessians' fire. He wheeled his mount and urged them forward again. This time it was the Hessians who fled.

Now Burgoyne had a hard time to keep his troops in

order. The British army was soon in full retreat. But the guns on Bemis Heights, firing steadily on the Americans, discouraged any follow-up. Arnold took in the situation at once.

If the redoubt commanded by Colonel Francis Breymann could be captured, the Americans could safely pursue the retreating British. The victory would be complete if the British were caught before they retired behind their fortifications. He called to some Connecticut troops, "Come on, boys, if the day is long enough, we'll have them all in hell before night!"

They followed him as he sped onto Freeman's field. There they were stopped for a while, but Arnold, disdaining all danger, passed through the hail of bullets safely to General Ebenezer Learned's brigade. Urging them on, he led them against two fortified log cabins and silenced the guns inside. They left the rear and side of the Breymann redoubt exposed. Hardly pausing, Arnold yelled to the nearest soldiers, "Follow me!" and they came on the run.

The infantry scrambled over the walls, and Arnold waited confidently for the gate to be opened, but before he could reach it, his horse leaped into the air, mortally wounded.

Crashing to earth, Arnold did not feel the pain at first. But when he tried to get up, he found his left leg was shattered. It was the same leg that had been wounded at Quebec. The fight raged on, and the redoubt was captured by the Americans. But the man who had led the successful attack lay on the ground in agony—not only agony of body, but agony of mind.

He realized that he might be a cripple for life after this. That would mean no more fighting, no more exaltation on the battlefield, no more cheering from his men. The feeling of absolute power would be taken from him. What would happen now?

He looked up to see Major Armstrong standing beside him. "General Gates," Armstrong said coldly, "orders you back to quarters, sir."

8

The battle came to an end with darkness. Burgoyne had been defeated. There was no longer any danger from his army. Arnold knew that, but it gave him no comfort. "I wish that bullet had pierced my heart," he said bitterly as the stretcher-bearers carried him away.

The surgeons were determined to amputate his leg, and he bent all his energies to defying them. It finally exhausted him, and he lapsed into unconsciousness. But his fury had impressed the doctors. He kept his leg.

He did not keep his peace of mind. Always fretful when inactive, he was ridden now by the most terrible doubts. Would he ever be able to walk again? Was he to be a cripple for life? If he did recover, would he ever be able to fight again?

Why was General Gates rewarded by Congress with

a gold medal, while he, who had led the assault to victory, was ignored? When would Congress restore his rank? For three and a half months these thoughts tortured him as he lay in the Albany hospital. Then, with his shattered leg in a massive cast, called a fracture box, he set out for home.

Only the last question was answered at this time. There was so much pressure on Congress to give the hero of Bemis Heights some sort of reward that they finally authorized General Washington to restore Arnold's rank of major general. But now no word came from General Washington! Wondering if he were out of favor with the commander in chief, Arnold found something else to worry about.

It was late January, 1778, before Arnold heard from Washington. His commission was enclosed, and there was a query on whether he would be well enough to serve in the next campaign. It was probably pique that made Arnold wait for weeks before he replied. Then he said he was not yet well enough to serve in a physically active capacity.

He gave proof of his disability when he went, by slow stages, to Valley Forge in Pennsylvania that May. He came to renew his loyalty oath to the United States, an oath that he was to break in the near future.

The Patriots were in high good humor. It was obvious that the British were soon going to have to evacuate

Philadelphia, and only the previous month the welcome news of an alliance with the French had arrived. Young French officers were already in evidence—promise of help to come.

Washington saw at a glance that Arnold was, indeed, not yet fit for active duty, and he decided that as soon as the British left Philadelphia, he would install Arnold as military governor there. There was bound to be a certain amount of disturbance and upset in a city that had been occupied by the enemy and was now returned to American government. It was also the seat of both the Pennsylvania Assembly and the new country's Congress. Neither of these bodies had got on well together in the past, and Washington was sure that the city would need a strong man to rule it. That man, to his mind, was Benedict Arnold.

When the British received orders to leave Philadelphia and march to New York, it was because of the new French alliance with the United States. Clinton's army was to be depleted by 8,000 men, who would be sent to the West Indies in an effort to capture French islands there. The Patriots were happy, since that meant there would be that many fewer men to fight.

Arnold marched into Philadelphia in June, while bells clanged, guns boomed a salute, and people cheered. Not all the people were cheering, however. A good number of citizens had remained loyal to the king, and they had thought they were safe while the British occupied the city. Now they wondered what was to become of them.

One of Arnold's first moves was to close all the shops, proclaim military law, order all Loyalist stores seized, as well as the British Army supplies left behind. All excess goods of certain kinds belonging to private families had to be reported.

This last made people furious. The man they had welcomed so heartily was soon considered an autocrat, if not a dictator. If they had known that Arnold, using his power as military governor, had made arrangements for the sale of much of these goods—the money to be shared between him and two co-conspirators—he would have been despised as well.

The flaws in Arnold's character, which had been hidden when he faced hardship and danger, came to the surface now—not completely to the surface, of course, for he was wily enough to keep them out of sight, and to make his dishonest deals without signing his name. The desire for power, the desire for a high place in society, and the desire for money rose within him. There was little to stop them. They had gnawed at him from within; now they were able to come a little into the open.

When Arnold moved into the elegant John Penn House, people began to wonder. His private fortune was small and getting smaller. His pay was negligible for the upkeep of a mansion like the Penn House. More than one sober citizen began to question how Arnold could afford such luxury. Then he bought a coach-and-four and put his servants in livery. Surely, people thought, he could not possibly afford all this! *Where* was the money coming from?

The money came from a number of deals, in which he at once became an active partner. He used his power to clear vessels from the port of Philadelphia, so that they could transport the flour he had bought so cheaply to the West Indies. There it would bring a high price. Using the government's money to buy it in the first place meant that when the profits came in, he could repay the government. He made a great deal of money this way without putting out any of his own.

He ran into trouble several times. People not only suspected what he was doing, but began to try to prove it. When he heard there was a British raid on Egg Harbor, where one of his ships had a valuable cargo, he used wagons and waggoners from the American Army to unload the cargo and bring it safely to Philadelphia, where it could be sold.

Later he had to stand court-martial for some of his offenses—this among others—but he managed to wriggle free each time with no more than a reprimand from his commander, George Washington.

And now his urge for riches had received a new impetus. He had met Peggy Shippen and wanted to marry her.

Peggy was one of Judge Edward Shippen's three daughters. She was her father's favorite and knew it. The youngest of Shippen's three girls, she was also the most spoiled, perhaps because her interests were close to her father's. She did not care for art or literature. She found business fascinating and absorbing and, if she had been a man, would have found scope for her talents in this direction.

But she was, instead, a rather fragile-looking blonde, with delicate features and a flirtatious air. She was only eighteen when Arnold met her.

Peggy's father had tried to remain as neutral as possible during the war, living quietly, and trying to keep from being involved with either the Tories or the Patriots. Peggy was ardently Tory, not so much because of her political beliefs, but simply because the English Army officers were more polished and gave more lavish parties than the Patriots.

When the British withdrew from Philadelphia, she was very depressed. Where would the good times come from now? Her father had not made money under either regime, being so determined not to be associated with either one. Their house was getting shabby, although it was one of the finer mansions in the city. She wanted new gowns, gay entertaining, and her father would not hear of it.

When Arnold moved into the Penn House, the young beauties with Tory sympathies perked up. When he bought his coach-and-four and began entertaining lavishly, their spirits revived. Here was a man who knew how to spend money! They cared not all where it came from or how he had got it. The main thing was that he knew how to be extravagant.

From the first time he saw Peggy Shippen, Arnold was caught by her dainty blond beauty. He sensed in her the same fierce pride that he had, the same determination to get what she wanted from life. Although she played a flirtatious game, now seeming to bend toward him, now drawing back, he knew that she would be his prize someday. The main difficulty lay in persuading her father to permit the marriage.

Edward Shippen did not like Arnold. He was not a "gentleman," as Judge Shippen understood the term. Arnold was old enough to be Peggy's father. He was a widower with three growing sons. Yet there was nothing tangible on which Judge Shippen could base a refusal to let Arnold court his daughter. Although Arnold first proposed marriage in the fall of 1778, Peggy agreed when her father asked her to wait until spring before making a decision.

It was surprising that she agreed, for Peggy Shippen

was accustomed to having her own way in most things. If she were refused anything, she would promptly go into a fit of hysterics and not be calmed until her wishes were granted. Yet in as important a matter as this, her possible marriage to Arnold, she seems to have agreed to wait a few months. Was she aware that she might be marrying someone as ruthless in satisfying his personal wishes as she was in satisfying hers?

Whatever the reason, she waited until April of the following year, while Arnold sent her lovesick letters and prepared for his forthcoming marriage by buying a handsome mansion on the Schuylkill River, called Mount Pleasant. He also saw to it that his two older sons were packed off to school so that there would not be too much of his family to disturb the bride. Hannah, his loyal sister, stayed with him, but she may have had misgivings about sharing the housekeeping with a young and fashionable belle.

It is interesting to note that the school to which he sent his sons was run by a Tory minister. This is only one of the small items which began to show how he was turning from his allegiance to the Patriot cause. His bride-to-be had Tory sympathies. He had not hesitated to give passes through the Patriot lines to ladies who wanted to go to British-held New York. Ostensibly, they were going there for the purpose of shopping, but letters could easily have been carried that way. Indeed, he had given so many passes at one time that General Washington had asked him to stop the practice.

But there was a deep and abiding resentment buried within Arnold. Perhaps it was even more than resentment, for it burned with a steady fury. He had not been properly rewarded for his great endeavors. He had been sneered at by Congress; he had been passed over in promotions, while lesser men—in his opinion—received the higher ranks. He had been spied on, lied about, and accused of base things by men who had stayed safely at home, while he had lost his health and personal fortune in the fighting.

These were his thoughts. His shady deals were justified in his mind because they helped to repay him for what he had lost. His dictatorial attitudes not only were natural to him, but were a reaction to the accusations which began to be hurled at him. It doubtless pleased him that he was marrying a Tory girl, and setting her up in a household maintained by ill-gotten money.

But there was something else, too. He really *was* in love with Peggy Shippen.

9

While Arnold had been courting his Peggy and trying to become a rich man by any means whatsoever,
his enemies had not been idle. He had never been one
to watch his words or be suave in his actions, and many
people had been offended by him in one way or another.

The Supreme Executive Council of Pennsylvania was
headed by Joseph Reed, a man who hated Arnold. This
hate came to a boil over the affair of the British sloop
Active. The story is a strange one, and Arnold's part in
it shows the two sides of the man.

Four Connecticut men had been fishing at sea, when
they were overtaken and captured by the *Active*, which
had a crew of nine. The Patriots did not take this
meekly. Eventually they managed to overpower the

British and confine them belowdecks, after which they steered for New Jersey.

The British, however, were resourceful. They melted pewter spoons and made bullets. Then they pried up the hatch and fired at the Americans, who, though wounded, turned the swivel gun on the British. Forced below once more, the British jammed the rudder so that the ship could not be steered.

Hunger and thirst did what the Americans could not do, and at last, the British seamen had to release the rudder. With Yankee determination, the Americans steered for New Jersey again. They were almost there when they were overtaken by a brig. This time it was an American ship, but it belonged to the State of Pennsylvania, which claimed three-quarters of the prize money.

The Connecticut men protested. They had fought and bled for the prize money they would get for that sloop. Pennsylvania denied their claims.

At this point Arnold came into the picture. He was indignant that good fighting men from Connecticut should be treated so shabbily. He advanced them money to fight for their rights and managed to arrange that the case come before Congress. On the other hand—and here was his greedy side again—he gave them the funds on condition that he should get half the money awarded them and also that they should keep his name and the fact that he had made this arrangement with them entirely secret.

This move won him the undying enmity of Joseph Reed. The states were not closely connected in those days. Each one was inclined to consider itself first, and each one distrusted its neighbors. Pennsylvania, more than most, feared a central government, which would strip the state of much of the power it now possessed. Perhaps one reason Arnold went into the *Active* case as readily as he did was that it was Pennsylvania that had blocked his promotion to major general.

Arnold's reputation was such that his monetary interest in the *Active* case was suspected almost at once. People who knew of him were apt to ask, "Why is *he* so interested in this case? What is *he* going to get out of it?"

Philadelphia was the nation's capital. It was also the capital of the State of Pennsylvania. Joseph Reed's council was furious when Congress refused to oust Arnold from his position and even more angry when they were asked to present evidence of his "crimes" to a Congressional committee for investigation. The council did not have enough evidence. It was sure that Arnold had acted against the public interest, but it could not prove it.

The fight raged back and forth. When New York State representatives offered a large tract of land to Arnold as a reward for his bravery, he had instant dreams of fortune. He saw himself as a wealthy landlord, owner of thriving villages and farms. He had set out for Washington's headquarters in New Jersey, when the Pennsylvania council printed a proclamation listing all its accusations of Arnold. It sent it to Congress, to all the state governments. It was published in the newspapers.

Arnold was angry enough to give up his New York dream and hurry back. He demanded a court-martial, but that would have meant that he was to be judged by the military. The civilian forces, led by Reed and the council, opposed this bitterly. After weeks of controversy in the newspapers, Congress decided that Pennsylvania had no right to the *Active* prize money, and the Congressional committee cleared Arnold of the civilian charges. Washington would deal with the remaining two—one of which was the accusation that Arnold had used Army wagons for his own purposes.

Benedict Arnold had no fear that he would be condemned by Washington, but he had had enough of the wrangling and suspicion in Philadelphia. He resigned his command there, and on April 8, 1779, he married his Peggy.

Almost at once he began thinking of ways by which he could change over to the British side in the war. There seems little doubt now that Peggy had a good deal to do with this new decision. A spoiled young girl, she had been exceedingly eager for a gay social life. This had been the lot of her elder sisters, and everyone had agreed that she would be even more beautiful than they. Instead, the war had started between the colonies and England, and life in the Shippen household had become very uncertain.

Since Judge Shippen had refused to ally himself with either side, he was suspected by both. Fearful of mob outrages, he had moved his family out of their handsome brick home, with its formal gardens and its orchards. They had spent some time in Amwell, New Jersey, where he made a futile attempt to farm. When that became too dangerous a spot, the Shippens went back to Pennsylvania to the Falls of the Schuylkill. Surely, Judge Shippen thought, they ought to be safe there. He journeyed into Philadelphia each day so that his house would seem to be occupied.

First, their retreat was discovered by American troops, and Peggy, her nose in the air, thought them a ragged rabble. When they marched away, the whole family breathed easier. Then the troops came back—this time in retreat from the Battle of Brandywine. Peggy was quite cheered. The British had won. Perhaps her troubles would soon be over.

When the news came that the British were occupying Philadelphia, she felt triumphant. Now, at last, she would come into her own! And so she did, as soon as the swaggering British officers spied her.

She was soon flirting with the most attractive of them—Captain John André was one of them—and gracing the balls and parties, the concerts and plays. When her father, determined to be as neutral with the British as he had been with the Americans, tried to make her economize or forbade her a new gown, Peggy promptly had a fit of hysterics, which always brought Judge Shippen to heel.

For her entire childhood, Peggy had used these hysterical tantrums to get what she wanted. She would scream and weep until she had her way. It was a childish thing to do, but she continued the practice into womanhood, seeing that it worked very well for her.

Her new British friends had no difficulty in persuading Peggy to become Tory in her sympathies. She had already decided for herself that life was pleasanter by far under British rule than it had been under the Americans. She had only to think back on her dismal life on the Amwell farm or the lonely, uncomfortable house at the Falls of the Schuylkill to make the decision. And besides, the aristocratic officers of the British Army knew so well how to flatter a woman.

When Benedict Arnold moved into Philadelphia as the military governor of the city, Peggy was afraid that all the good times would disappear. But then Arnold moved into the Penn House and began to entertain as lavishly as the British officers had. He did not question a lady's political beliefs—it was enough if she was beautiful and well mannered and knew how to flirt delicately. Peggy and her little group of friends—all Tory belles—were soon riding the crest of Philadelphia society again.

Once she and Arnold were married, she must have realized how easily he could be persuaded to become a turncoat—to change his allegiance. If he seemed about to forget some of the slights and insults he had received at the hands of American Patriots, Peggy was on hand to remind him of them.

Congress owed him money but did not want to pay until the stories of his graft had been investigated. It owed him his back salary, as well as money he had advanced for supplies on the hazardous trip to Quebec. He also declared that he should have been paid commissions on the commissary funds he had handled. Congress' reply was that he had been accused of appropriating Canadian property and selling it for his own benefit.

In her subtle way, Peggy was able to keep Arnold's resentment at white heat. It was not long before he began to make an attempt to get in touch with General Clinton, the British commander in New York.

10

It was not an easy matter for an American general to start a correspondence with Sir Henry Clinton. He could not send his letters through the mail because there was no exchange of mail between the two enemies. He had to find an intermediary. But who was eager enough to serve the Tory cause? Who could be trusted not to betray him to the Americans? Who would be brave enough to run the gauntlet of both the American and the British armies?

Peggy came up with the answer. The crockery man, she said, would be perfect for the job. His name was Joseph Stansbury, and he liked to write poetry. Peggy was sure of his loyalty to Britain, because she had heard him mentioned by several of the British officers who had been her escorts. He might be able to explain his travels as being business, and it would be easy enough for him to come to the Arnolds for instructions, since they had bought their china from him before.

But there was another difficulty. General Clinton was a man who kept to himself and his intimates. He would not be willing to see a mere dealer in crockery and china. There would have to be a go-between in New York—someone who would be accessible to Stansbury, yet who was close enough to Clinton to bring the message to his attention.

"Why not Captain André?" Peggy asked her husband.

"That poet? That painter of stage scenery?" Arnold asked scornfully.

"He is a fighter, too," Peggy told him. "But more than that, he is Clinton's aide, and I heard that only last week he was put in charge of British intelligence." Arnold knew, from her smile, that she had had this news from one of her Tory friends.

And so Stansbury was sent for. Closeted with Arnold and Peggy, he was questioned and probed. At last, satisfied that his loyalties were with Britain and that he would not betray them, Arnold and his wife gave him a message for Clinton: General Arnold was offering his services to Clinton, either by "joining the British army, or by cooperating on some concerted plan with Sir Henry Clinton," as Stansbury wrote later.

Stansbury managed to find his way to New York undiscovered, and there he turned to a friend, Jonathan Odell, who, like Stansbury, liked to write poetry. Odell had been a British Army officer and later had become an Episcopal minister in New Jersey. He had had to flee to New York and was very bitter on the subject of the Patriots.

The two of them got to Major André and brought the astounding message that General Arnold was willing to change sides in this revolutionary war. André rushed off to his commander, Clinton. Neither one of them could really believe that the message came from Arnold. Were they being fooled? Who was behind this astonishing offer? On the chance that it was bona fide, they arranged to send a reply, but they worded it so that they did not commit themselves to anything.

In Philadelphia, meanwhile, Arnold and Peggy went through anxious days, waiting for a reply. The waiting was not made easier by a letter from General Washington, saying that Arnold's court-martial had been postponed for a month, perhaps for two. This news did not make Arnold regret his step, but he must have been tortured by doubt. What if the British did not accept his offer? What if he were condemned by the court-martial? What if he were disgraced in the eyes of everyone?

When Stansbury came back, he brought André's reply. It startled Arnold, who had thought that he could simply desert to the British and that when he did so, countless American soldiers would follow him. He had been cautious enough, however, to say in his message that if this should not be the case and his American possessions should be confiscated, the British would have to pay him for his losses.

André's reply indicated that the British wanted much more than desertion from the Patriot Army from Arnold. The general was to pretend that he was still a Patriot so that he could make possible the seizure of a large body of men; he should send on information of a military nature; he should try to persuade other American generals to go over to the British; he should assist anyone who was stirring up the population against the Patriot cause; and he should try to return Burgoyne's army to the British by means of an exchange of prisoners.

Arnold was set back on his heels. His vanity had been sure that the British would welcome with open arms a man of his fighting stature, yet they had completely disregarded his offer to change sides openly. They wanted him only as a spy. To make matters worse, they had not mentioned any specific payment for his services, although he would be running grave risks in order to give them.

Stansbury brought him a dictionary with instructions for a code for future letters to André. The British had a similar dictionary, and the code was to be written in invisible ink above the words of an innocent-sounding letter. The code above these words was to be numerals, indicating the page, the line, and the word in the dictionary. Each letter was to be marked somewhere with an *F* or an *A*, to show whether the ink used was to be brought out by fire (heat) or by acid.

Writing such a letter was not an easy matter. First the real message had to be written out; then the words of the message placed in order throughout a seeming business letter so that it could be read by the one who received it. At the same time, the business letter had to make sense. Arnold and Peggy spent a great deal of time over each letter that they sent to André.

But Stansbury did not want to carry their letters every time, and a complex method of communication had to be worked out. It was never easy to send these letters, and some of the messengers between Arnold and André had a dangerous job.

The bargaining between Arnold and the British went on for months. The British hammered away at Arnold, urging him to get a command which he could betray to them. But they refused to name a sum of money which would be paid for this.

Arnold was a trader. He was not going to commit himself without knowing what his reward was to be. He did not realize that the British High Command was not even certain that it *was* dealing with Arnold.

With several go-betweens, it was possible that the British were dealing with someone else—even with the American spy system!

At last André proposed that they meet somewhere under a flag of truce. Then everything could be discussed in person, and there would be no possibility of misunderstanding. But by this time six months had gone by, and nothing had been accomplished. The British moved southward to besiege Charleston, South Carolina, and André went with them. The negotiations between him and Arnold were cut off for some time.

It was not until December, 1779, that Arnold's long-delayed court-martial took place. Although the Americans could not know it at the time, he lied strenuously in his defense, denying that he had profited by the closing of the stores when he first took over the military command of Philadelphia.

He lied again when he said that he had never done anything against Washington, for he had just sent information about his commanding general to the British a short time before. He lied easily and convincingly.

Only two counts were rendered against him at the trial, and these brought a rather mild reprimand from Washington. Even that irked Arnold. He did not want to be blamed for anything—even if he *had* done wrong!

Since he had resigned his command at Philadelphia, Arnold no longer had the chance to make easy money.

88

He and Peggy moved into a small house that her father owned and tried to cut down expenses. But both of them were now used to living on a lavish scale. Arnold racked his brain for ways to make money.

Prize money might be the easiest, he thought. He was used to the sea and the command of ships. He wrote a letter, asking to be given command of a fleet of frigates to harry the British shipping (and collect prizes) until he was fit enough to rejoin the Army. The Board of Admiralty refused his request.

Then he approached the new French minister. Putting his request in a stilted and roundabout form, what he really asked for was a loan, for which he would serve the French. Apparently Arnold would promise to serve any nation that would pay for his services.

The French minister refused, of course. The refusal was bad enough, but it was underscored by a little talk on ethics. And to add insult to injury, in Arnold's mind, the French minister was staying in Penn House, where Arnold had known his most prosperous days. Rather than listen to what the Frenchman said, Arnold rudely left.

In later years, Arnold often advanced a reason for his betrayal of his country. It was the fear, he said, that the French alliance would result in America's becoming a subject state to the French. But there is little doubt that his hatred for the French, which had started in Canada, received a tremendous impetus at this time.

There was only one chance left, only one way to recoup his fortunes. That was, as Arnold now saw it, to make every effort to obtain an American command in order to turn it over to the British. His mind turned to the strategic forts of West Point, which André had mentioned sometime before. He saw treason as the only way out of his financial difficulties. It is typical of him that he did not recoil from the idea but set out at once to pull the right strings.

11

Several important men spoke for him and told Arnold that Washington had listened to their suggestions with courtesy. Sure now that the coveted post would be his, Arnold began to make preparations for his contemplated betrayal. For some time he had been quietly transferring some of his assets to London. Now he tried to sell his New Haven house.

He stopped to see Washington at headquarters in Morristown, New Jersey, but the commanding general gave him no specific encouragement. Still, Arnold was hopeful. He went back to Philadelphia again, limping with a cane and with a high heel on his shortened leg which he would have to wear for life. But on his way home he visited West Point, casting a practiced fighter's eye at the weak points in the defenses there.

On his return, Arnold found Philadelphia agog with the news that the French fleet had arrived in Rhode Island. If Sir Henry Clinton tried to blockade it, he would need to draw away many of the troops in New York. This would be Washington's chance to recapture the city. In readiness for the coup, Washington had his troops at Tappan.

Arnold saw his chance. Notifying Congress that he was about to rejoin the Army, he got them to vote him $25,000. He probably laughed to himself at the thought that they were paying the man who was about to wreck their new country. Then he set out for King's Ferry, not far south of West Point, where Washington was moving his troops across the Hudson River.

Arnold rode up to the general, saluted smartly, and said, "I am reporting for duty, sir."

Washington was pleased to have the fighter at his side again. He knew Arnold's value as a leader of men in battle. He knew that Arnold was one who could encourage and stimulate his troops. He said, with satisfaction, "I am giving you a post of honor. You will command the left wing of the Army. . . ."

Arnold's features remained expressionless, but he paled until his startlingly blue eyes were the only color in his face. He turned away without thanking Washington.

Pacing back and forth near Washington's head-

quarters, Arnold was careful to limp heavily. When asked what troubled him, he said that he was afraid he was not strong enough to go into battle. He could scarcely mount his horse. He would much rather have the post of commandant of West Point.

Everyone was surprised. Arnold, the fighter, asking for a safe post? It didn't seem possible.

In Philadelphia, Peggy waited eagerly for word from her husband. When, at a dinner party, she learned that Arnold had been given command of the left wing of the Army, she had one of her fits of hysterics. But as always, she recovered her wits sooner than others. She let it be known, in a subtle way, that she was fearful for her husband's safety. She had hoped he would be given something less dangerous.

Her hopes were fulfilled on August 3, 1780, when Washington, very much disappointed by the change in Arnold, granted his request, and gave him "command of the garrison at West Point."

The change in Arnold went deeper than his American associates could imagine. Clinton had set aside 500 pounds to be paid Arnold for information he had *already* given the British. And Arnold had offered to surrender West Point to them for 20,000 pounds even before he left Philadelphia, in the hope of getting the West Point command.

Now that he had been given the coveted position,

Arnold went quickly to work. He decided to live in the house of Beverly Robinson, a Tory in the British Army. The house was across the river from West Point, which was very much in its favor.

Since Stansbury would no longer be able to serve as a go-between, he would have to find someone nearby. It was not long before he settled on a wealthy farmer, Joshua Hett Smith, who lived near Stony Point. Smith had done a little intelligence work for the Patriots, but he was not too much trusted since he had a brother in New York City who was a strong Loyalist.

This suited Arnold exactly. He flattered the young country squire and drew him out until he expressed himself willing to help Arnold arrange for a "peace" between the two factions that were tearing the countryside to pieces. Arnold was able to use Smith as a courier, sending a letter to André in New York to arrange for a meeting between them.

Meanwhile, missing Peggy and their baby boy, he sent for them. One of his aides was dispatched to bring them north to West Point, and Arnold wrote out minute instructions for their care and safety.

The answer to his letter to André was so long in coming that Arnold grew worried. He always wrote in code and signed himself "Gustavus." He referred to himself as a merchant and to André as "John Anderson."

Hoping that he would soon have a visit from André,

95

when all arrangements could be settled, both military and financial, he told Colonel Elisha Sheldon, who commanded an outpost at North Castle, to be on the lookout for "John Anderson," who was to be sent to Arnold as soon as possible. He implied that Anderson was one of his intelligence agents.

Arnold inspected West Point and its defenses, making lists of the weak places as if he were about to have them repaired. Since there was too large a garrison which might resist the British, he sent 200 men to Fishkill to cut wood for the winter. They would be easy enough to capture, for the 20,000-pound price for West Point was to include 3,000 men and the fort's stores.

He was told that the great chain, stretched across the Hudson to stop any British vessels that might try to sail toward the fort, had a weak link. This he ordered removed, and the links on either side tied together with rope. Of course, this would offer no resistance to British ships, but he carefully sent off requisitions for a new link, knowing that it would take more time to make the link, transport it, and install it than he needed.

He was carefully and methodically making things ready for the great betrayal. Only one thing disturbed him. He had had no answer to his letter.

And then, on September 10, André's reply reached him. It came in a peculiar fashion, for André had written directly to Colonel Sheldon at North Castle. He signed himself "John Anderson" and said he would be meeting his friend, Mr. Gustavus, the following day under a flag of truce sent out from Dobbs Ferry.

The letter was delivered to Arnold by two young officers, who had brought it to him because Colonel Sheldon was ill, and they did not understand what the letter was about. Arnold explained quickly that John Anderson was one of his agents, and that he was Gustavus. But he was angry to think that André had been careless enough to mention the time and place of their meeting.

His anger did not last long. He was too excited. Things were beginning to move now and move fast. Within a few days he would become a wealthy man. Undoubtedly, he would be knighted for his services to Great Britain. The future ahead of him was rosy with promise.

12

That very day Arnold ordered his personal barge to be readied and was rowed downstream for some miles. He spent the night with Smith and went on the next morning. When he neared Dobbs Ferry, he saw the *Vulture,* an English warship, in the river, and his blue eyes narrowed. Undoubtedly, this was the ship that had brought André from New York.

Suddenly, from a sheltered cove, there came the sound of shots. A gunboat that had been hidden from sight streaked out into the river and came toward them. It was a British gunboat! Two or three others, hovering near the *Vulture,* sprang into action and began to give chase to Arnold's barge.

There was nothing he could do but order his men to retreat. He dared not show a flag of truce. He would have been unable to give any reason for it to the Americans. He told his men to pull the barge about and go upstream again.

At Tappan he paused long enough to give a note to one of the soldiers there. "Take this to General Washington's headquarters at once," he said. In the note he stated that he had been surveying the river for places to put beacons and signal guns in case of an enemy attack. This would explain his presence on the river that day.

But he was angry inside. What sort of fool was this André that he had not warned the men on the *Vulture* about Arnold's coming? When dusk fell, he went back to his house across the river from West Point, seething inside. He would never do this again! André would have to be the one who risked his neck the next time!

He did not know that André was patiently waiting at Dobbs Ferry but waiting inland so that he could not be seen from the river and that he waited in vain all through that day for Arnold.

Now Arnold knew he would have to move fast. The next time, the rendezvous *must* take place. There was too much involved for waiting, and there was too much danger unless things were properly arranged.

He began copying reports which the English would be happy to have: reports on the defenses at West Point, the supplies, the number of men, the amount of artillery and the positions of the guns. He copied papers relating to the war which had been under discussion at Washington's recent council of war. He copied all these carefully on very thin paper so they would be easy to carry in concealment.

There were six of them. Six thin sheets of paper which were to hang a man . . .

Peggy arrived at last. When word came that she was at Smith's house, Arnold went by barge to meet her there. Now that he had his family, he hastened to write André. His letter arranged their next meeting at a place which he was wise enough not to mention. He only said that he would send someone to Dobbs Ferry, by water, to pick up André and lead him to a safe place for their rendezvous. The date was to be Wednesday, September 20, 1780.

The man he planned to send was Smith, and they were to meet at Smith's house. Smith's family was away, and the house would be vacant that night and available for the meeting. Smith also agreed to take the letter addressed to "John Anderson" to New York and deliver it to the intermediary there.

When Arnold and his Peggy reached the Robinson house, which was to be their home for such a short time, they found a note from General Washington. The commander in chief was going to Hartford to meet the French admiral and requested a guard of fifty men from Peekskill.

Now, at last, things seemed to be working out for Arnold and his plans. Washington would be out of the way while he conferred with André. He was delighted when Colonel Beverly Robinson, the Tory owner of his house, wrote asking if he would be allowed to come and discuss the confiscation of his property. Since the letter came under a flag of truce, Arnold had to read it to those who were sitting with him at dinner when it arrived.

Everyone there—except Peggy, of course—thought it would be very unwise to see Robinson. It would put Arnold in a peculiar light! It was a matter for the civilian authorities, not the commander of West Point!

Arnold kept his face impassive, but he boiled inside. Because Robinson had included in his letter the code name of the New York intermediary, Arnold knew that the "business" would have been the betrayal of West Point and would have had nothing to do with the house he was occupying. It would have been so easy to meet with Robinson here at his headquarters. It was going to be difficult to meet André at Smith's house.

He took the letter with him when he went to meet Washington, who was to have an escort of fifty dragoons from West Point. He found the same reaction in Washington. It would do his name no good to deal with a Tory on civilian matters. "Let Congress attend to it," Washington said.

Well, it would have to be André, not Robinson then, Arnold thought, riding back from Peekskill to his temporary home. But it would have to be soon, for he had learned one thing that might bring him even greater reward from the British: Washington was planning to stop at West Point on Saturday or Sunday and would stay with the Arnolds!

What a prize he would be! The commander in chief of the Patriot Army, the one man whom all factions in the quarreling colonies revered for his steadfast honesty and devotion! The one man who had managed to keep the Americans fighting for the past five years!

The next few days were frantic ones for Arnold and for André. Their plans to meet went astray or were delayed, and it began to seem that the meeting would never take place. Everything conspired against them: Smith's lighthearted incompetence, the difficulty of sending letters via a flag of truce without Arnold's aides knowing the contents.

For the second time the meeting between Arnold and André did not come off. On the night of September 21, André waited on board the *Vulture* for Smith to arrive, but Smith, who had ridden a good deal that day, was tired, and his tenant farmer, Samuel Cahoon, was unwilling to row him out to the British ship in the Hudson.

Smith finally persuaded Cahoon to carry a note to Arnold, explaining why he did not have André at his

house. Arnold did not get it until morning and, infuri-
ated at the way things were going, determined now to
carry matters through by himself. He called for his barge
and had himself rowed downstream to Smith's house.

There he ran into another snag. Smith had been unable
to get a boat in which to bring André to shore from the
Vulture. Naturally, Arnold could not use his own barge
—it was manned by soldiers of the Patriot Army. But he
did requisition another boat and sent his bargemen to
get it. He indicated that he would need it for Smith,
who was to go on a secret mission for him that night.

Once more Smith tried to get Cahoon to row him to
the *Vulture,* and once more Cahoon refused. It was
evening when Smith brought the farmer to Arnold. The
general tried to persuade Cahoon to row down to the
British ship and bring off "a secret agent." The farmer
tried to get out of it. He did not want to go at night,
and he did not want to go alone.

"This meeting *has* to be at night," Arnold said, trying
to conceal his impatience.

"And if you don't want to go alone, get your brother
to go with you," Smith added.

The brother was fetched, but he, too, was unwilling.
Finally Arnold resorted to threats, and Smith gave them
some strong drink to bolster their courage. They set out
at last, with Smith as passenger, for the *Vulture.*

André had about given up hope when they reached

the British ship. He was impatient to be off and flung a long cloak over his uniform. By the time the two farmers had rowed back upstream to the meeting place, several miles downriver from Smith's house, Arnold was already there and waiting.

For several hours the two men discussed their plans in the dark. Arnold, with his mind on reward, tried to get as much money as he could for his treason. André coolly refused to agree to pay Arnold a large sum of money if the plan failed. He would be repaid for his losses and he would retain his rank—in the British Army instead of in the American—but the 10,000 pounds that Arnold asked for, no matter what happened, was refused.

Then they got down to details. Arnold had copied everything—reports, a map of the West Point defenses— and now they discussed strategy for the taking of the fort. It was dawn before they had finished. There was no chance to get André back to the *Vulture* without being seen. Besides, the two farmer brothers were proving stubborn again. And there was still more to be settled.

"We'll go back to your house," Arnold told Smith, "and finish our talk there." The boat was sent northward with Smith, and the two conspirators rode horses. They had to pass inside the American lines before they reached Smith's house, and André was careful to keep covered by his long cloak so that his British uniform did not show.

They were at breakfast when they heard the firing of cannon. From the bedroom where they had been talking, Arnold and André could see the *Vulture*. An American shore battery was shooting at the British ship. Her rigging and quarterdeck hit, the *Vulture* had to head downstream for safety.

The two men looked at one another in astonishment. This was an unexpected development. Now André would have to go some distance to rejoin the ship.

When they finally came to terms, Arnold told André that he would have to change to civilian clothes if he did not want to be shot by some American soldier. He folded the reports and maps which he had copied on thin paper and stuffed them inside André's stockings. Then he wrote out passes, so that Smith could take André back to Dobbs Ferry, where the *Vulture* was probably safely anchored.

Arnold bade the English officer a quick farewell and left for his home. All the way northward, Arnold's quick brain was scheming, scheming. The British were to attack on the twenty-fifth, a Saturday. He would be the brave commander, ordering his men about. But they would be sent to the wrong places at the wrong times, and there would be such small numbers sent that they would be captured. He knew that the British could get

106

into the fort easily enough. There were so many weak places in the walls, and he had pointed out all of them to André . . .

Peggy was waiting for him when he arrived. She saw at once, from his face, that the final arrangements had been made. Now there was nothing to do but wait. The waiting was hard.

13

On the twenty-fifth, Washington, who had spent the night at Fishkill, started for the Robinson house. He was to have breakfast with the Arnolds, but he stopped on the way to inspect some fortifications. Not to disappoint Peggy, his hostess, and keep her waiting, he sent on two of his officers to start breakfast with the Arnolds, but when they arrived, Peggy was still upstairs.

Arnold sat down with them for a while, then went into the pantry. There he found an officer and a tired soldier who had just arrived from North Castle, an outpost of the Patriot Army.

Arnold took the letter they handed him and opened it, intending to give it a quick glance. The words leaped out at him from the paper with their bad tidings. Lieutenant Colonel John Jameson had written:

"I have sent Lieutenant Allen with a certain John Anderson taken going into New York. He had a passport signed in your name. He had a parcel of papers from under his stockings, which I think of a very dangerous tendency. The papers I have sent to General Washington."

The "papers" were those he had copied in this very house! They were in his handwriting! Arnold repressed a shiver.

There was a second document. Arnold opened it, wondering what further terrible news he might find. It said that Anderson had been returned to South Salem, another outpost.

With a monstrous effort of will, Arnold said to the officer, "You will wait for a reply." Then, trying not to seem to hurry too much, he went outside, ordered his horse saddled, and sent word to have his barge ready at the landing.

Only then did he race upstairs to his Peggy. He had no time for a lengthy farewell. He whispered to her that they had lost, that everything had been discovered, and he would have to flee. A knock on the door startled both of them. It was Major David Franks, one of his aides, to tell them that Washington was almost there. Peggy fainted, and Arnold, waiting until Franks left, ran out of the house.

He hurled himself onto his horse and tore for the

landing, sliding down a steep ravine to save time. His bargemen jerked their heads up as he thundered onto the little dock, unfastened his saddle, and threw it into the barge. Then he jumped in himself.

"Pull away for Stony Point!" he cried. And when the men stared at him in astonishment, for he was obviously upset, he added that he wanted to get back in time to meet Washington.

He sat in his barge, issuing nervous orders for more sail and scanning the river in back of them for signs of possible pursuit. Then, when the barge neared Stony Point, he suddenly announced that he had to see the captain of the *Vulture* on Washington's business.

The men hesitated. It was clear that they did not believe him, and Arnold said quickly that he would give them two gallons of rum. This offer changed their minds, apparently, and they continued downstream.

At the *Vulture*, Arnold climbed aboard to be greeted with consternation. The officers who had accompanied André had assumed that the barge was bringing him back. When they learned that André had been captured, they were angry. Clinton, they knew, would be terribly upset when he heard what had happened to his friend.

Arnold was unconcerned about André. He felt he should have been welcomed aboard; he felt the British were lucky to be getting the services of a brilliant, admired general like himself. To prove how popular he was with his men, he walked over to where the American bargemen were talking with some British sailors and offered to make them noncommissioned officers if they would desert to the British cause.

They looked at him in surprise. Then, as he continued to exhort them, they turned away in disdain. Their General Arnold was nothing but a traitor! Furious, Arnold ordered them thrown into the brig as prisoners of war.

When Washington arrived at the Robinson house it was midafternoon. The treasonable "papers" that Colonel Jameson had referred to were handed to him. Washington was stunned. The man on whose bravery and loyalty he had counted had betrayed both him and the country he fought for. It was a terrific blow.

To make matters worse, one of Arnold's aides had a high fever, and the other one was completely distracted by Peggy's hysterics. She wept and shrieked and pleaded for mercy, even before the aide knew what had happened. But as was always the case with Peggy's hysterical fits, she did not give away herself or her part in the plot. The men who surrounded her in that house were convinced that she was the innocent victim of Arnold's crime.

It seems incredible that Arnold, on his part, should have thought that the British would entrust him with something important now that he was openly on their side. Once a traitor, always a traitor (to the highest

112

bidder) was undoubtedly their reaction. Yet his ego was so pronounced that he apparently expected, from the beginning, to be given a command at once. He was full of plans, but no one listened to them.

Clinton was shocked by André's capture. Surely Arnold could have saved him. But Arnold, it would seem, had been more concerned with saving himself. Clinton insisted that Arnold write Washington on André's behalf, taking much of the blame for André's capture.

André was tried on September 29, 1780, and condemned as a spy. The young British major had thought he could choose the manner of his death if he were found guilty and was shocked when he was informed that, being a spy, he would have to be hanged. He kept his equanimity surprisingly well during the days of his imprisonment. Perhaps he felt, in his heart, that his good friend General Clinton would manage to release him in some way.

General Clinton was certainly trying. He insisted that Arnold write another letter—a threatening one this time —but it had no effect. Clinton himself sent emissaries, proposed a mediation board of two foreign commanders, one of whom was with the American Army, the other with the British. The Americans replied with silence or refusal. But once, when a Patriot colonel had delivered some papers from Washington to Clinton, he suggested

114

casually that if Arnold were turned over to the Americans, André would be freed.

It must have been a great temptation for Clinton, who was eager to save his friend. But the policy of never returning deserters was ironbound. He could not do it. The same suggestion was hinted at another time but failed to produce results.

Indeed, the Americans were very anxious to have Arnold in their hands. He had struck a devastating blow at Patriot morale by his desertion. Always admired by his soldiers, he had done something unforgivable. He had deliberately toppled their idol—himself. And he had done it for the basest of reasons—money.

Major André, on the other hand, was admired by the Americans for his calm acceptance of his fate and for his courteous manner. To the end he hoped for some exchange of prisoners which might free him. There could be no exchange, because he had not been captured in his uniform, so he was not a prisoner of war. Instead, he had been wearing civilian clothes. There was no other way to regard him but as a spy caught behind the American lines.

It was Arnold who had insisted that he change to those clothes. It was Arnold who had insisted on bringing him back to the Smith house, which was within the American lines. But Arnold was free.

The Americans hanged André on October 2, 1780. He met his death bravely, to the admiration of those who saw him. There were tears shed for him by his captors, but no one shed a tear for Arnold, safe in New York City.

The grand dreams which Arnold had had were crumbled to dust. General Clinton wanted nothing to do with him personally, for he could not forget that Arnold was responsible for the death of his friend. He appointed Arnold a brigadier, but he did not give him a command.

His unfriendly attitude was not lost on the other British officers, who also ignored Arnold. They felt he was not their social equal either, while the Tories in New York were sure he had deserted to the British for the money he would get. He was snubbed on all sides.

14

The British were bound to feel that they had had the worst of the bargain. They had agreed to take Arnold, but what they had wanted was West Point. Now the American stronghold was safe, and they were burdened with a sulky American general who had a price on his head. To make the situation even more difficult for Arnold, the hanging of André as a spy had turned Clinton against him.

Yet after Peggy had been forced by the Pennsylvania council into exile and had rejoined her husband, Clinton realized that perhaps there had been no further desertions from the Patriot Army because Arnold was being kept in idleness. Clinton sent him then to Virginia, with orders to raid the plantations and the towns and to keep the Virginia militia occupied. This would relieve the

British General Lord Cornwallis in South Carolina.

Arnold did not know that Clinton did not trust him. Several other officers had been told to take the command from him if anything suspicious developed.

Once he was back in the field, some of Arnold's surliness lifted. But although he took Richmond by surprise, without any resistance from the Patriots, burned tobacco warehouses, and destroyed a good deal of shipping, he no longer seemed to take the joy in combat that he once had. He slept with pistols by his side, well aware of the fact that his life would be worth nothing if he were ever caught by the Americans. He cannot have failed to hear of the many times he had been hanged in effigy by indignant Patriots. He did not want it to happen in actuality.

Peggy received him on his return with the subdued air she wore these days. She could not forget that he had failed, that she might have been really wealthy and a member of the peerage, petted and admired by the English nobility. *If* Arnold had not failed! That failure she found hard to forgive. As ruthless as her husband in her planning, she was not, however, suspected too much. Her face, rather emptily pretty, was that of a girl. Who would think her capable of the same treason as her husband—a middle-aged, embittered cripple?

That fall Clinton began receiving reports that indicated Washington was about to join the forces in the

South. As matters stood, with part of the American armed forces in the South and part in the North, neither section was very strong. Clinton did not want them to become strong, and to prevent their joining, he decided to threaten to attack New England.

Arnold was given the command of the expedition. He sailed up Long Island Sound with thirty-eight ships and hundreds of men, bound for New London. This would be home territory, and he probably felt a grim satisfaction in returning there as leader of an invading force. All his life he had felt unappreciated by his neighbors. Now he would "show them"!

He landed his troops on both sides of the Thames River at night. Those on the western bank marched into the city at dawn without difficulty and were soon looting happily. They were given firebrands and told to destroy the public buildings and stores. One of the warehouses must have contained gunpowder, for suddenly there was a great explosion. After that, the fire leaped from house to house. New London was largely destroyed.

The soldiers on the eastern bank of the river had not been so successful. They launched attack after attack on Fort Griswold without success. Counting his losses, Arnold decided to order his men to retire, but before his messenger reached them, they had managed to enter the fort.

The American commander surrendered, only to have

his own sword thrust into his breast. As if it were a signal, the British troops, remembering the numbers of dead they had left outside the fort, gave no quarter. It was a massacre of the Americans.

The people of New London now were in no danger of forgetting Arnold. Their hate was deadly, and Clinton finally realized that to send Arnold out against the Patriots only roused their antagonism and made them stronger.

In Virginia and again at New London, the change in Arnold was easily seen. He no longer charged at the head of his men, eager to lead and encourage them by his own example. Even this had been taken from him because of his treason! He was too well aware of his vulnerability. If he were wounded and captured, nothing would await him but a hangman's noose. Nowadays he stayed well in the rear to save his skin.

As soon as Cornwallis had surrendered at Yorktown and the American Revolution was officially at an end, Arnold and Peggy and their children sailed for England. Arnold, as usual, was full of plans. He hoped to get Clinton's command and began to cultivate the people he thought might be of help in his ambition. He took a house and bought a carriage and was well received by the king.

Unfortunately, he had not counted on the power of the Whigs in England. They had been against the war with the colonies from the beginning, and now that the war had been lost, their power was strengthened. The Tory government fell, and Arnold was reduced to the rank of retired colonel—on half pay. That hurt. It was lucky for the family that Peggy had been given a pension of 500 pounds.

Once more Arnold had to turn to trade. He bought a brig and set out to make his fortune all over again. He was not well received in Canada but built a store in St. John, Newfoundland, and traded with the West Indies, just as he had done when he was a young man.

Peggy and his children, as well as Hannah, his sister, joined him there. And it was Peggy who now began to be the bulwark of the family. Despite her rather exaggerated femininity, Peggy had always been interested in business and finance. Her father had taught her a great deal, and she had shown much more business sense than his only son.

She put this ability to good use in managing as much of the family's income as she was allowed to. But Arnold, as always, was a gambler. He never could resist the chance of large returns on a small investment, and the result was that all too often he not only lost the small investment, but had to borrow money to make good on his failures.

They went back to England when the French Revolution occurred, and war between England and France seemed inevitable. Here was his chance to become a famous general, Arnold was sure! But he was not listened to. He was not given a command. He was insulted publicly, and fought a duel with an English lord, who so despised him that he disdained to fire at Arnold when Arnold had fired and missed.

He went back to the West Indies, where trading had become really dangerous now, the French and British islands being so close together. Once he was captured and thrown into a French prison ship. What strange twist of the mind lay behind the fact that he gave his name as "John Anderson," the name André had used in their correspondence? Was it because the French had sentenced him to be hanged?

He made an extraordinary escape from the French prison ship and managed to reach a British ship, where he would be safe. Then his dangerous speculations began again. He made money, and he lost money, but the losses were usually greater than the gains.

Peggy's hysterical fits grew longer and more severe. It is hard, at this distance of time, to decide whether they were real or splendid pieces of acting. She raged and screamed, but she never seemed to lose her business sense. She had a passion for appearing to be far wealthier than they were, and this and the necessity to provide for her and the children (they now had a daughter and four sons) drove Arnold to further speculations.

Peggy did not approve of his speculations, which she knew would prove ruinous. She tried to restrain him, tried to get him interested in safer ways of making money, but as Arnold grew older, his schemes for achieving glory and money became wilder and wilder. He would not listen to her, and his final investment in a privateer was a complete disaster. This seems to have been the blow that felled him. He died, a disappointed, embittered failure in June, 1801. He was sixty years old.

Peggy survived him for only three years. In those years she struggled to put his affairs in order, to leave something for her children. She managed to pay all of Arnold's debts before she died. Perhaps this was her atonement for her share in Arnold's treason.

Fiercely egotistic, always reaching avidly for glory and for wealth, Benedict Arnold died forgotten, shamed, and poor. Little that he had schemed for had turned out as he had planned it. His life was a waste of power, of intellect, of passion. If he had not been so cold-blooded in his treason, one could easily pity him. But he is denied even that.

Index

124

The Author

CATEAU DE LEEUW was a successful portrait painter when she turned to writing for young people. Since then she has published almost half a hundred books, including novels, nonfiction and poetry. Miss De Leeuw lives with her sister Adele, also a well-known author of juvenile books, in Plainfield, New Jersey.